AF483641

About the Author

Janet Sipl is an acclaimed educator who has a passion for teaching. She taught in elementary school for over 30 years, and was honored with the National Teacher Training Institute's "Teacher of the Year" award. She also taught at Baldwin Wallace University.

This lifetime of teaching has prompted her to create and share this amazing interactive book combining reading and mathematics. It is designed to capture and hold a child's interest, which in turn establishes a positive and successful learning experience.

Note From The Author

I created this book to help children learn to add in a fun interactive way. Learning to add makes the connection between "the number of objects you start with" then increasing that number by "more objects" to get a "total number that includes all objects". Research has shown that addition is important because it is the first big mathematical step after early learners build their basic number sense.

The book also puts into practice the skill of repetition. The repetition of seeing, hearing and saying a concept or word out loud is a fundamental learning tool that not only encourages mastery of new skills but provides a sense of security and confidence through its predictability.

The bright, colorful images combined with the interactive repeating text and addition activities are a winning combination that will capture and hold your child's interest. Overall, "Amazing Addition: Learning To Add Is Fun", will increase your child's confidence and create a want to learn attitude during the process of learning to add. So sit back and relax while you enjoy this fun learning experience with your child.

As Always,

Janet Sipl

ADDITION VOCABULARY

NUMBER LINE

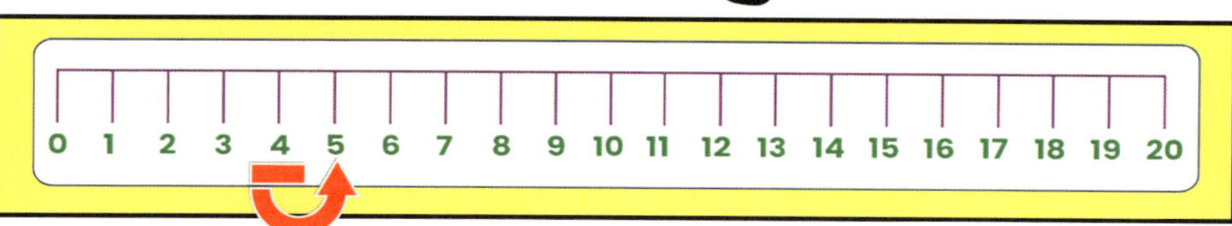

A READ AND LEARN BOOK

AMAZING ADDITION

Learning To Add is FUN!

Written and Illustrated by Janet Sipl

"Amazing Addition: Learning To Add Is Fun"
A Read And Learn Book
Copyright © 2023 Janet Sipl
All Rights Reserved
ISBN: 979-8-218-15992-4

1

One yellow duck,
by a red canoe.

If you add another duck,
you can count to two.

1 + 1 = 2

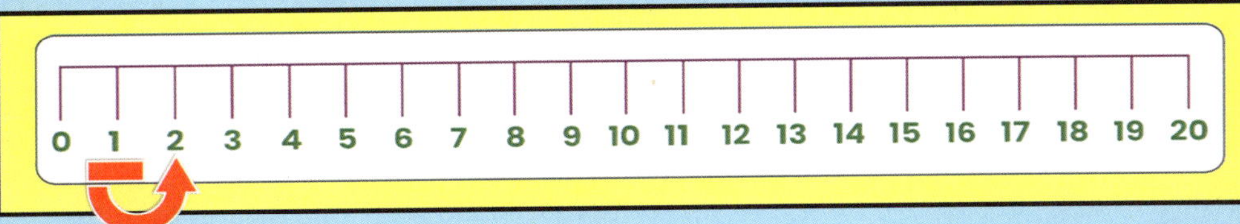

1 duck + 1 duck = 2 ducks
0 1 2 3 4 5 6 7 8 9 10 11 12 13 14 15 16 17 18 19 20

2
Two majestic tigers,
relaxing under the trees.

Add another tiger,
and you can count to three.

$$2 + 1 = 3$$

2 tigers   +   **1** tiger   =   **3** tigers

Three White Westies,
waiting by the door.

Add another Westie, and now you have four.

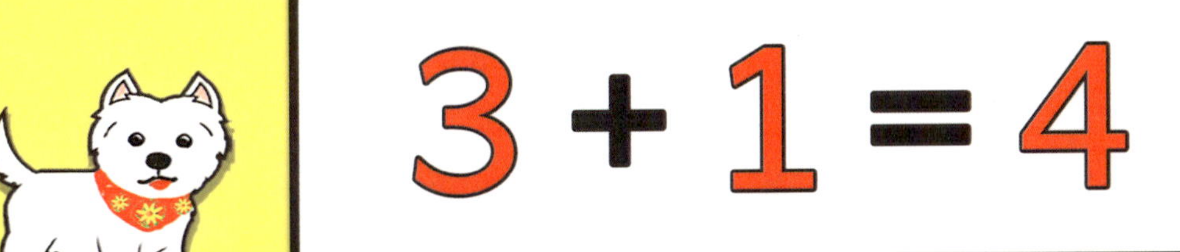

3 westies + 1 westie = 4 westies

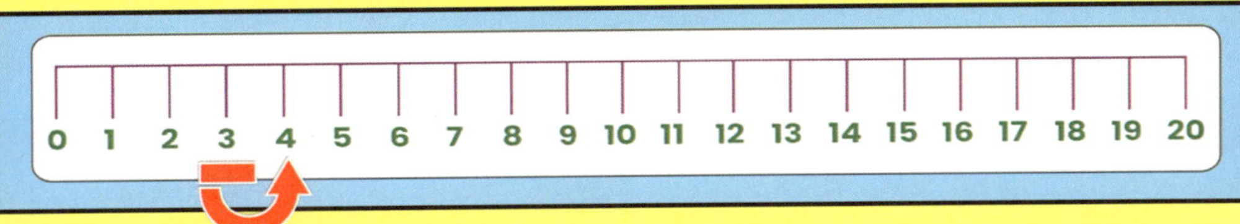

Four curious giraffes,
out for a Sunday drive.

If you add another giraffe,

you will have five.

$$4 + 1 = 5$$

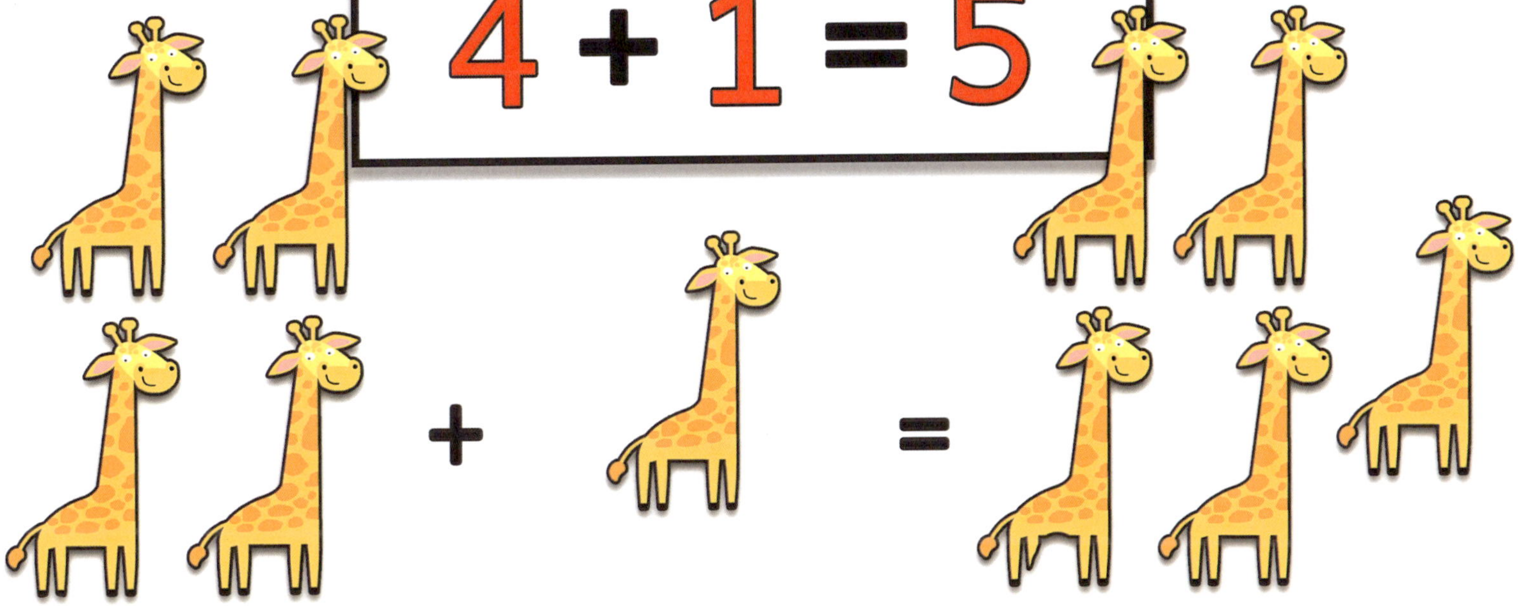

4 giraffes + 1 giraffe = 5 giraffes

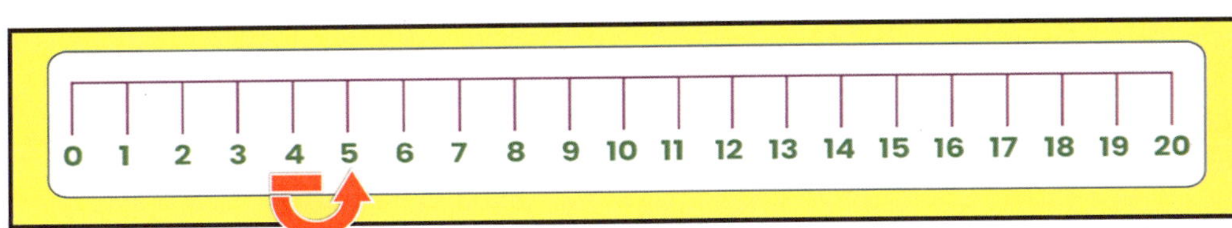

5

Five talented rabbits,
performing magic tricks.

Add another rabbit,
and magically there's six.

 +  = 

5 rabbits   +   1 rabbit   =   6 rabbits

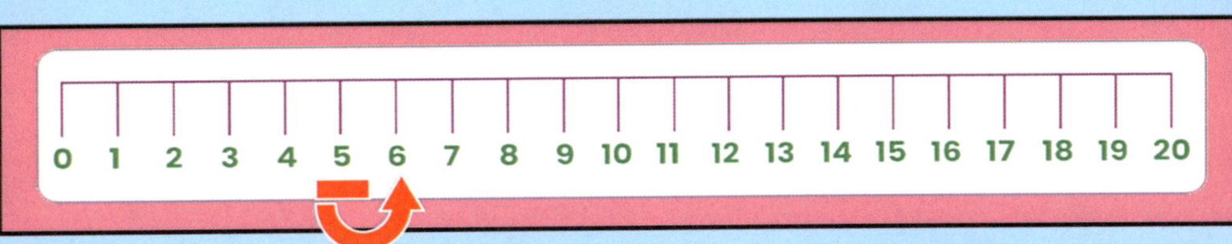

Six grumpy goats,
on top of Mt. Heaven.

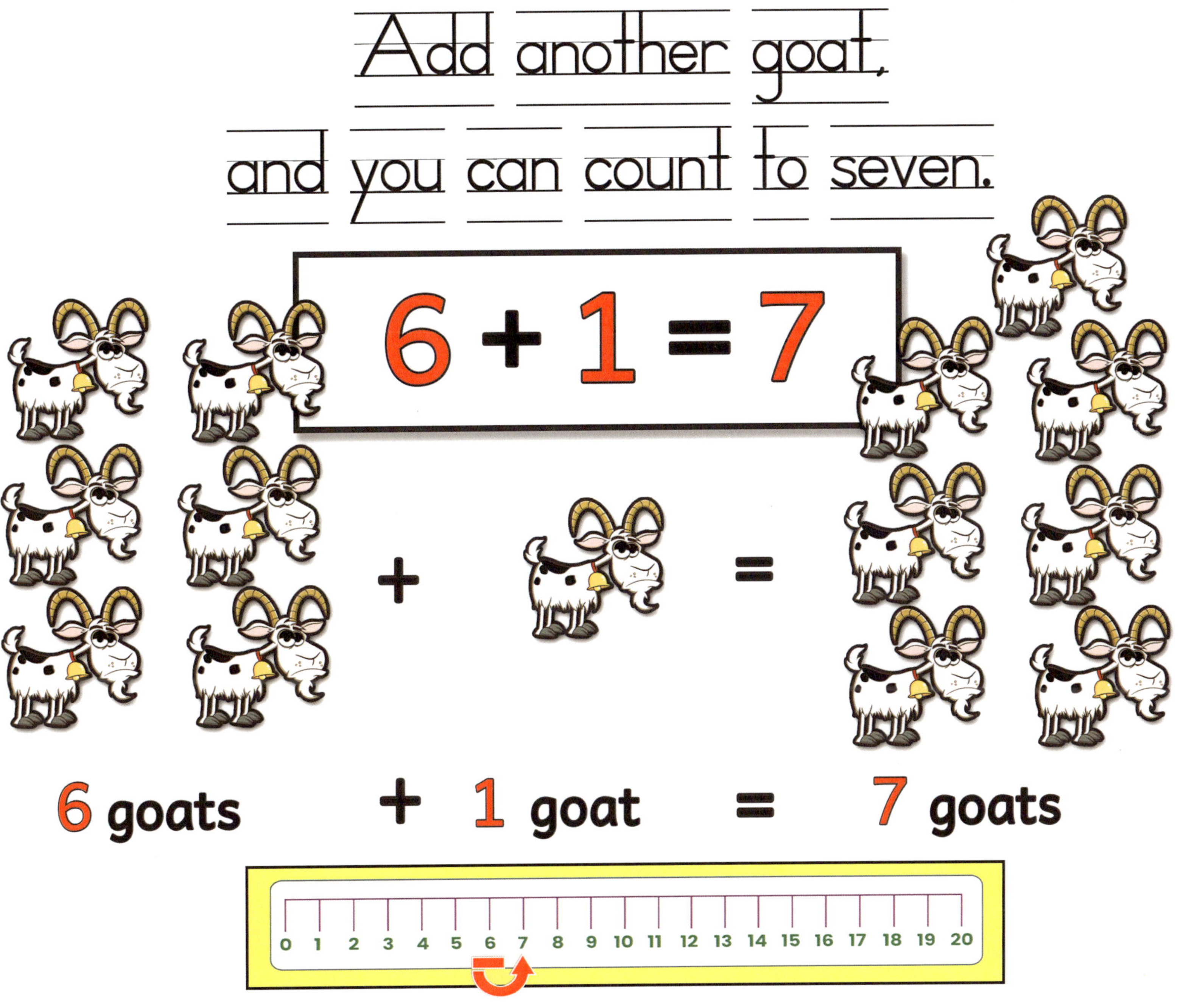

Add another goat,
and you can count to seven.
6 + 1 = 7
+
=
6 goats + 1 goat = 7 goats
0 1 2 3 4 5 6 7 8 9 10 11 12 13 14 15 16 17 18 19 20

7

Seven sweet pandas,

think bamboo tastes great.

Add another panda,
you now have eight.
7 + 1 = 8
+
=
7 pandas + 1 panda = 8 pandas
0 1 2 3 4 5 6 7 8 9 10 11 12 13 14 15 16 17 18 19 20

Eight funny frogs,
playing all the time.

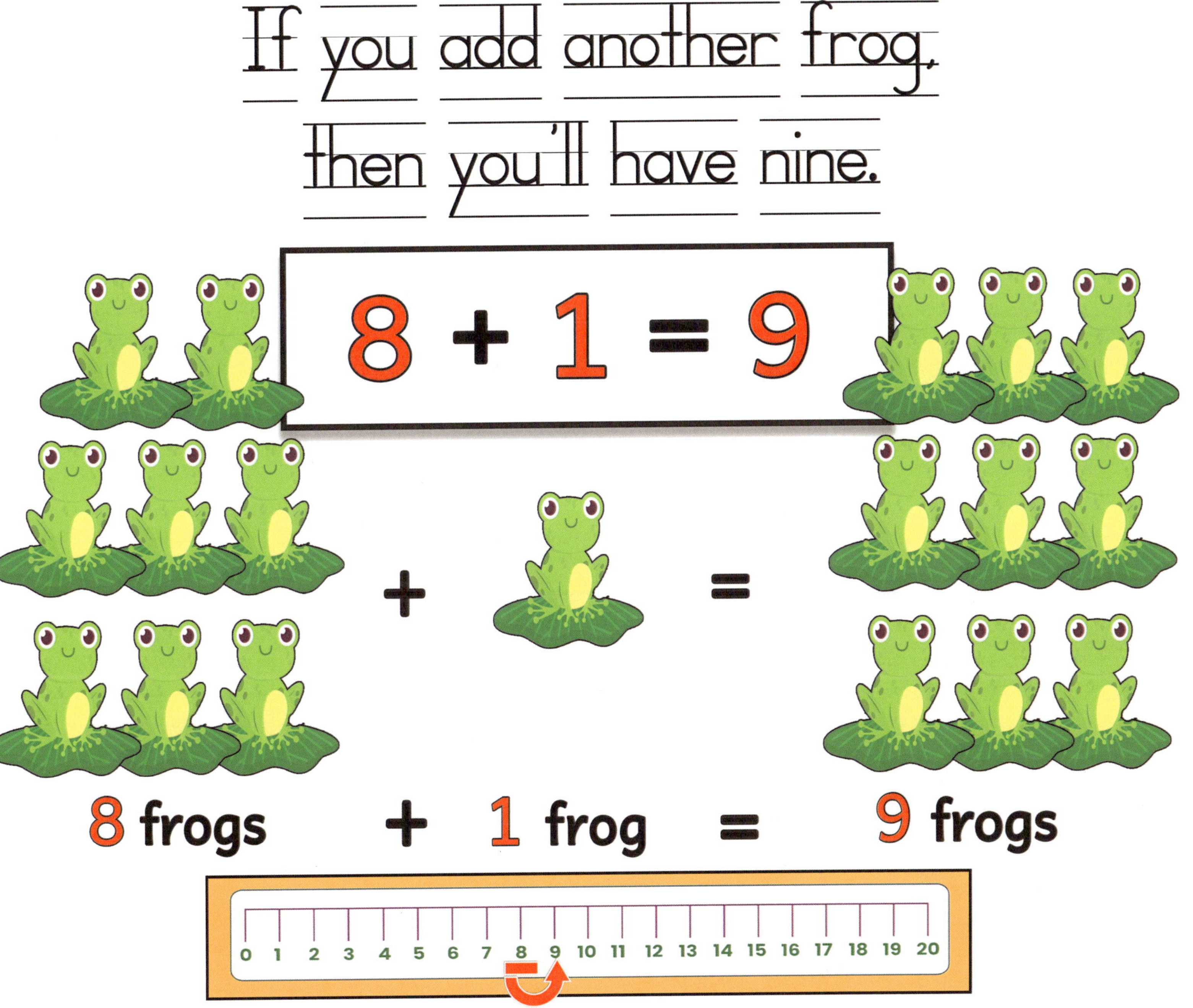

If you add another frog,
then you'll have nine.
8 + 1 = 9
+
=
8 frogs + 1 frog = 9 frogs
0 1 2 3 4 5 6 7 8 9 10 11 12 13 14 15 16 17 18 19 20

9

Nine chattering monkeys,
can be quiet now and then.

Add another monkey,
and you can count all ten.
9 + 1 = 10
+
=
9 monkeys + 1 monkey = 10 monkeys
0 1 2 3 4 5 6 7 8 9 10 11 12 13 14 15 16 17 18 19 20

10
SCHOOL
Ten amazing kids,
they are all addition pros.

You can add another kid,
just show us what you know.

10 + 1 =
10 + 2 =

Did you use the number line?
Try the one below.

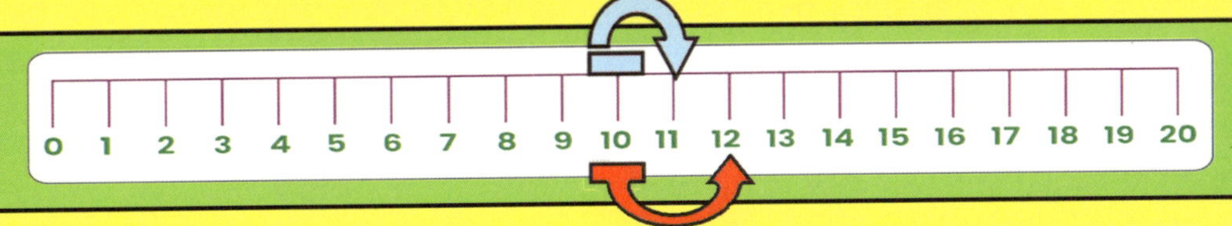

Parent Pages

In this book your child will be introduced to the concept of addidtion by using:

VISUAL OBJECTS

2 + 1 = 3

ALGORITHMS

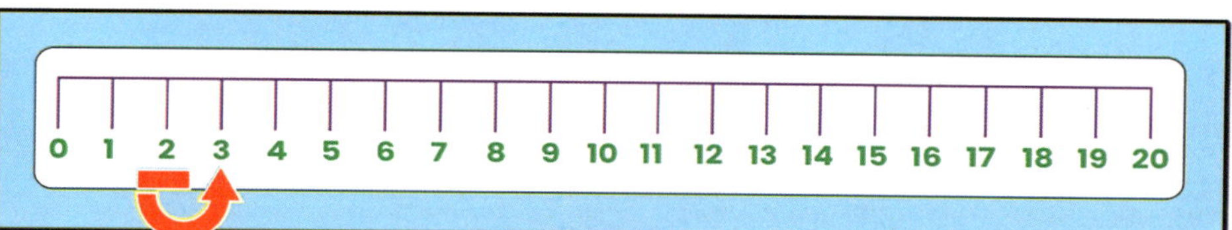

NUMBER LINE

To reinforce the concept of addition, have your child verbalize their thinking using their addition vocabulary as they are working through the process. Have them point and count the number of objects they are starting with, then emphasize that they are adding/plus one MORE, finally count the new TOTAL number that EQUALS ALL the objects. Focus on the fact that you are increasing the original number and coming up with a new *larger* total of *ALL* objects. This verbalization is of great importance when instilling the basic addition concept, and for helping with the instant recognition of addition facts to memory.

As a next step challenge, you will see that I have included a next level algorithm using plus 2.
Using a number line and objects of your choice, you can continue on with the next steps of learning to add.

1. Number **Plus 0:**   Example 2 + **0** = 2
2. Number **Plus 1:**   Example 4 + **1** = 5
3. Number **Plus 2:**   Example 5 + **2** = 7
4. Number **Plus 3:**   Example 6 + **3** = 9
5. Number **Doubles:**   Example **2** + **2** = 4
6. Numbers **Making 10:** What numbers add up to 10?   Example **6** + **4** = 10
7. **All remaining facts, including adding three numbers together**! Example **4** + **5** + **2** = 11

Make sure to use a number line to show and verbalize the process of what was done to get the answer, and please don't forget to write out the new aligorithm. This aligorithm visual is an important step in helping to assimilate addition facts to memory.

If you wish to continue to use the objects in the book and just add more of the same animals, I have included a copy of each animal and a 1-20 number line on the next page. This will allow you to copy and cut out additional visuals to use when counting.

_____ + _____ = _____

START

ADD

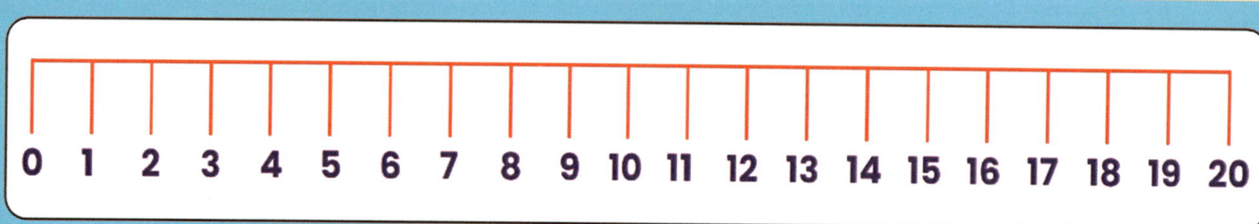
0 1 2 3 4 5 6 7 8 9 10 11 12 13 14 15 16 17 18 19 20

The Amazing Book Series:

Available online through Amazon, Barnes and Noble and other retailers.
(Type **Janet Sipl book** in the search bar.)

Read and Learn Series:

General Education:

Read and Rhyme Series:

Character Building Books

Find and Count Series:

STEM Books
(Science, Technology, Engineering, and Math)

IDIOMS, A TO Z ALPHABET BOOK

"Amazing Idioms A to Z, Alphabet Book,"
A Read and Learn Book

ISBN: 979-8-218-04125-0

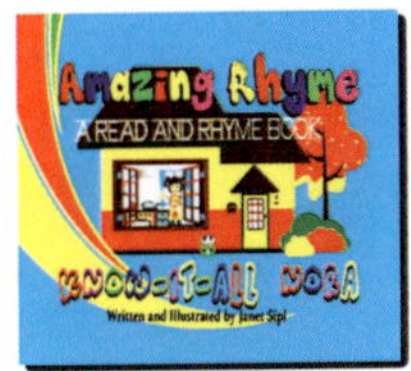

LISTENING & RESPONSIBILITY

"Amazing Rhyme: Know-It-All Nora,"
A Read and Rhyme Book

ISBN: 978-0-578-87734-1

MATH

"Amazing Numbers: A Find and Count Book"

ISBN: 978-0-578-72076-0

OPPOSITES

"Amazing Opposites,"
A Read and Learn Book

ISBN: 979-8-218-06197-5

SELF-ESTEEM

"Amazing Rhyme: The Curl,"
A Read and Rhyme Book

ISBN: 978-0-578-90264-7

SCIENCE

"Amazing Animals: Fun Facts and Animal Sounds,
A Find and Count Book"

ISBN: 978-0-578-81993-8

MATH-ADDITION

"Amazing Addition, Learning to Add is FUN!,"
A Read and Learn Book

ISBN: 979-8-218-15992-4

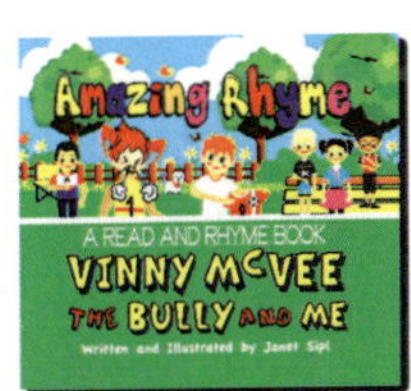

BULLYING

"Amazing Rhyme: Vinny McVee, The Bully And Me,"
A Read and Rhyme Book

ISBN: 978-0-578-94706-8

GEOMETRY

"Amazing Shapes: Having Fun With Geometric Shapes,
A Find and Count Book"

ISBN: 978-0-578-84823-5

DIVERSITY

"Amazing Rhyme: It's OK To Be Me,"
A Read and Rhyme Book

ISBN: 978-0-578-30791-6

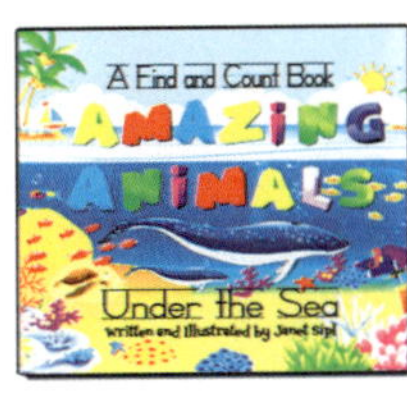

SCIENCE

"Amazing Animals: Under The Sea,
A Find and Count Book"

ISBN: 978-0-578-29426-1

JANETSIPL.WIXSITE.COM/BOOKS